Rumi Would Have Laughed

MYSTICAL LOVE POETRY

Winston Hampton

Sioux Ink
Fort Collins, Colorado

Copyright © 2015 Winston Hampton

Publishing House:

Sioux Ink
737 S. Lemay Ave, Ste. B4-156
Fort Collins, CO 80524
Yes@TraceeSioux.com
www.TraceeSioux.com

Book Layout ©2013 BookDesignTemplates.com
Cover Art by Chelsea Glanz, www.riseandshinearts.com

All rights reserved. No part of this publication may be reproduced, distributed or transmitted in any form or by any means, including photocopying, recording, or other electronic or mechanical methods, without the prior written permission of the publisher, except in the case of brief quotations embodied in critical reviews and certain other noncommercial uses permitted by copyright law. For permission requests and large quantity orders, write to the author Winston Hampton at William-hmptn@gmail.com.

Rumi Would Have Laughed/Winston Hampton. —1st ed.
ISBN 978-0-9907762-2-2

I dedicate this book to my Spiritual Teacher John Roger.

I was desperate to drink of the water of life, reading about it, hearing about it, the idea of it, the rumor of it was no longer enough, that's when my beloved friend, spiritual teacher and founder of the Movement of Spiritual Inner Awareness, John Roger, showed up. I first met him in a dream. With a firm, but gentle, hand he unwound the knots of my limiting belief, helped heal wounds from the past and brought in Light to dispel the darkness. For 35 years he has patiently shown me the Way, step by step, giving me spiritual tools and instilling the keys of Heaven into my awareness. He awakened me to direct knowing of the Divine. He is the most unconditionally loving person I've ever met.

I want a heart that is torn open with longing
So that I might share the pain of this love.
Whoever has been parted from his source
Longs to return to that state of Union.

—RUMI
The Rumi Collection, translation Kabir Helminski

Don't worry about saving these songs!
And if one of our instruments breaks,
It doesn't matter.
We have fallen into the place
Where everything is music.

—RUMI
The Essential Rumi, translation Coleman Barks4

Preface

When I write poetry I often wonder who is really writing it. From whence does it come? It just comes upon me. I get still and the first line comes. I do not know where it will lead. As the poem takes shape, it is my attempt to put words on some inner current coursing through me.

I really don't know much in a formal or scholarly way about the writing of poetry. It is likely that most of the mystical love poets didn't either. I have been deep in the study of the nature of beingness, the study of who we are, not as a mental pursuit, but as an experiential exploration, most of my life. Poetry is my translation of the Divine.

Since my awakening as a teenager, mystical love poetry has been a living thing. Even then, as I opened sacred texts, I found the words were a living energy that somehow came in through my eyes and began to make a circuit of energy all through me. I found myself transported to places the writer or poet had been when they wrote it.

Mystical love poetry expresses a state of consciousness, a state of being. I have always thought the great spiritual teachers and mystics to be the greatest of pioneers, willing to go beyond the reaches of the body, mind and emotions into the Great Nothingness, to the all abiding Oneness.

In direct communion with this Oneness the poet follows the flow. The Poet hears the song, the melody and then translates it into words. Like a symphony, first he hears the flute, *lets talk about the flute*, then she hears the cello, *oh my God, you must listen to the cello!* Then the violins, a whole group of sounds, like a flock of birds flying as one. The poet becomes the sound, becomes the symphony, is the instrument being played. Ecstasy!

I am madly in love with the great mystic love poets, Rumi, Hafiz, and Kabir to name a few. Rumi is a favorite, I deeply love Rumi! I reach out to many poets, authors and speakers to find the spell of their words. The words are the tracks which I follow back to find out who or what made the track, back to the essence of God.

This is the task of the poet. To leave a trail of breadcrumbs that others may follow, and in the following find something of great value. What makes a mystical love poet greater or lesser is how well they know the way to this upwelling source.

Back Home

Oh! Break Free! Break Free!
Crack the shell
Sails set for sea

Be born as a seed upon the wind
Oh! Pure Love
Oh! Dear Friend

Begin to wander, begin to roam
Begin to find your way back home

Become the sun, shining bright
Not just sun, but pure light

Fall my Love, with the rain
Let it wash away the pain

Flow and ebb with the tide
Love, my love, in love abide

~ Win as a teenager, 1974

Table of Contents

Preface i

Rumi Would Have Laughed 1

Oh My Beloved 3

You Are A Breath Of Fresh Air 9

Blessed 10

Who Has Been Made? 11

The Harvest 12

Know Love? 13

Karma 14

Wine Maker 15

Be A Revelation 16

Maker Of Us All 17

Sparkling Motes 18

Drunk In The Ocean Of Love 19

Sipping Tea 20

I Long For Your Embrace 29

Entering A New Kingdom 31

Garden Of Rumi	32
The Oil Lamp Is Empty	35
The Donkey?	36
The Flame That Does Not Burn	37
Inscribe It On My Heart	38
I Hurried Home	44
Wake From This Dream	46
Feet Dusty	47
I Asked For A Rose	48
Not The Laughing Corpse!	52
Beyond The Milky Veil	53
Do You Think You Breathe It?	54
Awakening	55
A Hidden Spring	56
This Living Cup	57
A Turning Point	58
Beggars & Saints	60
Halls Of Grace	69
Heavenly Sound	71
Butterfly Eden	72
Mecca Has No Place	73

I Know You	80
Wild Dreams	86
Thank You	91
Acknowledgements	92

Rumi Would Have Laughed

Rumi would have laughed
And he did
His grief spooned like sugar
Into the
Master's tea

A lazy full moon
Breasting the horizon
Mother's milk
To the blind

Come into the garden beloved
Come tea with me
We shall dance upon
The head of a pin

Yes, like drunken sods
We howl at the moon
And watch the echoes
Fill the empty places

We shall laugh
Like a wild river
Singing its song
On our way
To the ocean

Drowned in our cups
We howl
And disappear as drops
In this lovely sea!

Oh My Beloved

Oh my beloved
Twixt the beating of my heart
Lays a moment
Come to me in this moment
There is no tomorrow

This silence rings
With the sound of Your name
Which cannot be spoken

Yet in this eternal moment
You speak to me
Your honeyed words
Are nectar sweet

Oh my love
As I pause between my breaths
The bellows of my lungs sing
How is it I find
You standing here
Arms wide open
You take me in

Stars wheeling overhead
Moons yawning
Sunrise beckons
Where do You lead?

Oh lover of my heart
I hear the drum a calling
My heart is singing
A song of praise and life

And who am I
To be breathed this way?
What claim have I
To this pounding heart?

Oh Beloved One
I am quaking in Your sight
I am Your breath
Breathe me with ever such
Loving care

I cannot tell where You end
And where I begin
This circle lays unbroken
The love of which I speak
May not be spoken

To tell You how I love You
To let You know I see
My eyes are open
My words are rivers of light
In honor of You!

You Are A Breath Of Fresh Air

You are a breath of fresh air
In a challenging world
When you say, "thank you"
The sun comes out
When you say, "have a nice day"
Life becomes worth living
Or say, "you are beautiful today"
The angels begin to sing
Your words, "I love you"
Open the doors to grace!

Blessed

I am blessed
Who is this "I" who is blessed?
Is not the blesser also the blessed?
This song that has no sound
Keeps ringing
In my ears
Or is it my heart?

Who Has Been Made?

This impulse which beats my heart
A gift from the Maker
And who has been made?

The Harvest

In this womb of life
The Seed Maker plants the field
This field of humanity
This Gardener tills us
And furrows us up

The essence of the wine
Is in the field, in the seed
And in the vine

Have no fear
The Maker will harvest

Know Love?

Love is no miracle
The greatest wonder of all
Is how we live in the midst of love
And know it not

Karma

This One is the alchemist
Your shackles are golden cords
Like lotus blossoms
In the pond

Lift up your eyes
Shame is a gauzy veil
Easily torn to reveal
A winding stair

For our children bring answers
To questions we have not asked
Each one a passage
Home

Wine Maker

For reaped we will
And squeezed beyond measure
Trampled upon
Yet this is the blessing

You have only to see
With eyes of adoration
For the sifting and winnowing
As the wine is made

How sweet is this wine
Oh pour me out
For I am drunk beyond all hope
This essence of Spirit has overcome me

Be A Revelation

Here we are my love
We are gathered together
In a presence sacred and holy
Dare we be a revelation?

Our revealing is in
The essence of intimacy
Soar on wings of loving
Over the chasms of fear

That which we reveal
In our togetherness
Laid upon this sacred alter
Is now healed

For our one anotherness
Is this sacred essence
Where two (or more) are gathered
Revelation of wholeness

There is a great ring of marriaging
The ring of promise
of spiritual marriage

Maker Of Us All

Oh Maker of the field
Plow me
Oh Maker of the seed
Grow me
Oh Maker of the vine
Cultivate me
Oh Maker of the grape
Nourish me
Oh Maker of the harvest
Gather me in
Oh Maker of wine
Distill me
Oh Maker of my life
Open me
Oh Singer of the Great Song
Unstop my ears
Oh Essence of Loving
Let me drown
In Your great ocean

Breathless in my death
This ocean of wine
That I am drinking
This water of your essence
The wetness, the loving

Sparkling Motes

A star in the sky
One among many
Could feel lost
Amongst the multitude

And worlds without end
Depend on this sun
And myriad souls
Gather in its light!

All sparkling motes
In the Face of God
Particles or waves
Beyond the speed of light
This loving is!

Drunk In The Ocean Of Love

I am blessed
For I hear the song
The Maker sings
I am lost in the field
I have drunk from the cup
My heart has burst
I am no longer myself

Wandering wildly in the night
The moon and I drunk
In this ocean
Of love

Sipping Tea

I have found the One
In whom my heart delights
Sits with me here
Sipping tea

Says—let's walk beloved
For the garden is in bloom
The sun has smiled
And the clouds
Upon My sky
Set within the blue
Are for you
And your delight

Oh, dear Friend
You caught me at birth
And raised me
As my loving mother
And my giving father
Their love for me
Was Yours
You brought me here
To have tea
With You

The honey cakes
Melting on my tongue
So sweet
You, the honey of my heart
Poured in the goblet
Of me
Leaves me stunned
And gasping

And then the air
Of You
Comes pouring in
Swooned I am in You
You are the sweetness
As You gently and firmly
Breathe me

I have found the One
In whom my heart delights
This teacup is a door
A passage through proceeds
To the library genesis
Where upon
The parchment of the days
I'm shown
Your deepest intention

Each moment of my breath
Issues forth
An infinite heart
Known as love and mercy
Had writ upon it
My name

From the very heart of love
I have been made
Conceived and birthed
Like rays of sun
Streaming through the multiverse

Each day a letter
Each year a word
Each life a sentence
Has written forth
This most beautiful
Of poems
The story of me

I am your love poetry Beloved
Dance upon the waves
And sparkle in the sky
Are words upon Your lips
And as I speak
You issue forth

And know
This is all for you
This magnificent creation
I made for you of you and by you

Hark, now see
The varieties of love
Your darkest night
To purify you
That I may know Myself
This is my intent

Your sweetest moments
But a drop
Of the nectar of my love
Enter in now
And behold

You are
The one in whom
My heart delights
This bounty is yours
Come now
To the fountain
Climb into
The white marble bowl
All shot through
With glimmers of Me

Bathe your head
Let the cool living waters
Flow over and through you
Your agonies
But love misread
Build a line of your poem
Most beautiful
That are sung
In the highest courts

The king himself
As well as the queen
Now listen humbly
To your song
The altar of the Beloved
Is filled
With the pages
Of your days
And the candle there
Is the flame
Of you

The doors now open
Come now upon the step
Oh you in whom my heart delights
Enter in beloved
Yes, it is you
Come into the hall
Enter the throne
And take your place

Your golden crown
Was a gift by the Magi
At your genesis
For in the Ancient of Days
The council there
Proclaimed

Yea, the essence of good
The essence of the One
You are
Deliver forth into innocence
There to journey
And to return
Three treasures are yours
Crystal clear the path of your ways
A staff of royal purple
A rod, pure gold
These are Yours

The halls and rooms
Of this great school of mystery
Are built
With this living water
All the beauty in the world
But a glistening drop
On the cheek of your heart
And yet
All beauty is yours to behold

Do not delay
Open the sail sewed
From the fabric of love
For the wind is nigh
To carry you home

In joy the journey
Upon the billowing sea
Whitecaps blowing
Clouds scud across the sky
Waking once again
I found

The tea is still warm
Crisp and clear
On my tongue
As I sit
So blessed
Sipping tea
On this fine day
With the One in whom
My heart delights

I Long For Your Embrace

My heart blossoms
In your fertile soil
Your kiss inflames me
A mystery beyond knowing

Flames consume me
This burning rod
Glowing white hot
Penetrates me

Rest gently now
Warmed by the flame
That does not burn
In this home
Where you have always been

Entering A New Kingdom

I am entering a new kingdom
The right hand of loving
Gently gestures

The Traveler came for a visit
He moved in
The house is now His
I look into the mirror
I see the Traveler looking back

Garden Of Rumi

Rumi is still in the garden
Did you think him gone?
He laughs
Like any drunk
Who has landed
In a barrel of grapes

At the imposition
Of having to dig some
Hole in the ground
And fall in

Just to please these strange
Ideas of death
He just might do it
For the fun of it

Many who see the moon
Set into the sea
Believe it's now drowned
Never to return

If, like Rumi
You were on the other side
For you
The moon would be rising

Come now, into the garden
See the table is set
Tea is brewing
The Master is at hand

Take your place
For today
Like any other day in
The Garden of Rumi
He is here
Sipping tea
Holding concourse
With all these
Who have the moon
In their eyes
And Shams
The keeper of the Gate
Pours tea
With glee

The Oil Lamp Is Empty

How to live comfortably
On the head of a pin?
How to breathe
With no throat?
How to walk with no feet
And see with no eyes?

All glows from within
In this Kingdom of Light

Here burns a dancing flame
And yet
No wick is to be found
This flame burns on and on
Yet the oil lamp is empty

The Donkey?

The donkey was left at the border
The burdens were riches in disguise
Given to raise up the wretched

The path became a hall
This hall is now a house
This house is a home

We were home all along
On the table lay a feast
All this within
A flicker of the flame
A fire that does not burn

A gesture in the hand of love

The Flame That Does Not Burn

Rest gently now
Warmed by the flame
That does not burn
In this home
Where you have always been

Inscribe It On My Heart

The autumn leaves are turning
Bright colors so vibrant
The blue sky penetrates me
I have never felt
So all alone

I am lost
Where is the rudder
For this mortal ship?
I am desperate for some water
To fill this cup

All the sacred texts, incense
And prayers
Are not the light
To ignite this lamp

I long for my Companion
Knowing Your life
Pouring from
Your eyes
Illuminates my soul

This clay is only dust
Wet with living water
The birds taking flight
From the stoop
Of my mind
Have not the wings
To pass the sky

I long for Your embrace
You may send it through
My lover
Better yet, immerse me
In the sound
Of all life
Singing

How can I bear
Another moment?
I do not know
Where the door has gone
Wandering this desert
Thirsty beyond belief

Oh Travel Guide
I am in agony
Over Your absence
I yearn for the deep well
Of Your loving

Draw for me a map
Inscribe it on my heart
The living scripture
Never to be lost

Beloved Friend
Like waves upon
This shore of time
Crash again and again
Into me

A hollow reed I am
Press Your lips to me
That I may be
Your precious flute

I am afraid the colors of
The leaves or sky
Bright sunlit days
Will not carry me this time

The gulf in this abyss
Is too deep
Bring Your golden wings
Carry me across

Take me to Your breast
To thirst no more

I Hurried Home

I hurried home
Preparing tea
For the visit
With the Master
In the garden is silence

I waited at the door
For His appearance
Hoping to please
His Excellence
In the garden, flowers blossom

Anxious for His presence
I cleaned cup and saucer
Prepared the table
Listened for His knock
In the garden, fountains murmur

No one came
The front step is empty
Going to the garden for solace
I find Him patiently waiting
He has been here all along

Wake From This Dream

Oh my Beloved
I listen for Your voice
That I may follow You
And perhaps wake
In this living dream

This eternal moment
Is now my home
And these words are like
Clouds in the sky
Briefly they hold an image
Some profound truth
Then they dissolve

Feet Dusty

I encountered a great difficulty
On the way to the market today
As I wound through the streets
All that I had known
Began to leave me

I came upon a great emptiness
And became lost
All my plans so carefully laid
Fading smoke
All my learnings so diligently
Stored up, like worms
Quickly disappeared in the ground

When I reached the market
My belongings were gone
I could no longer tell
Who it was that reached
The market

Feet dusty
Throat thirsty
I awake

I Asked For A Rose

I asked for a rose
You gave me a bouquet
This bouquet of fragrance
Now a rose garden

I asked for a cup of tea
You brought the pot
With milk and honey
Fragrant and nourishing

I asked for a biscuit
You brought me a baker
With all her helpers
A full kitchen
And a mighty table

I asked for some water
Thirsty in the desert
Hot and tired from my long journey
Dusty and worn

You brought me a chalice
Filled with your word
Drinking deeply I awoke
From my mortal dream

A new dawn breaking
A golden pool
A bubbling spring so pure
Oh water of life!

How could I? This thirst?
Now quenched beyond measure
A glorious spring
Gushing from the heart of my chest

My life is an ocean
Of sweet and clear water
I am filled to the brim
My cup runneth over

I asked for a sip
You brought the sweet ocean
My thirst You quenched
Beyond hope or dream

Beloved Friend
You know for what I thirst
Better than I
My knowing is but a spark
In the fire of love

Awesome Your gifts
Surpasseth all measure
The return beyond
All request

I asked for a rose
You brought me delight
A fountain of joy
An ocean of loving
A return
Home

Not The Laughing Corpse!

Is it Armageddon?
Or simply milk cows coming home?
Tis the beating of my heart
Infallible, and everlasting
No, not the laughing corpse!

Beyond The Milky Veil

Oh, hallowed heart
You walk the skyways
Beyond the milky veil
That glowing stream of embers!

It is a simple story
Your beating heart

Do You Think You Breathe It?

The story of love
Not to be told
But lived
Beat by beat

The loving of the breath
Given freely
Do you think you breathe it?
Think again!

A gift of the Loving
Beyond the earthly veil
Breath given freely
Breathed by the One!

Awakening

As I looked in the mirror
An ancient and wise consciousness
Looked back

No need to kill my ego
Soul had simply enveloped it
And now my self-centered concerns
Had become self-supporting

Let the small self ripen
It will fall from the tree
All by itself

A Hidden Spring

A deep red rose
Velvety blushing
Sparkling drops of dew
Appears deep in the desert!

This Living Cup

This living cup
Described by breathing in
And breathing out
Suspended upon this moment

There is a gushing font
Forth from it comes a water
Never having begun
Never will it end

Bubbling forth a nectar
A honey so sweet
Living water that merely in its presence
No thirst may begin

A Turning Point

There is a turning point
A moment of meeting
A place where all possibility
Turns

The point where atoms rest
Within the molecule
Where whirling particles reside
With one another

Our earth held within the ethers
The solar system in the galaxy
The galaxy within a universe
Our universe within creation

Is not in the world
Though
Appears to be

Your breath becomes the link
Bridging this world
And the golden rainbowed realm of Light
The sound of your breath
Is the rushing wind

Turn now upon this point of love
Dive deep within this gushing love
Turn home into this heart of love

Beggars & Saints

I have my plans
For my life
I will do this
I will that
I will rise upon the stage
Success will be mine
I will have all this
I wish to attain

I will fall in love
I'll raise my family
My career will manifest
All I have long worked for
Will bear fruit

I will have my beautiful house
My routine will sustain me
I will be fit
My spouse will love me
I will build my house with care
And the world shall be mine

I will do as I was taught
Create the good life, for me
My life will be filled
With accomplishments
I will earn each dollar
And pay each debt

As the beggar walks the lanes
He pays for his meals by begging
To suggest a talk with angels
Is met with astonishment
What angels?
The Saints also walk the lanes
They walk with the angels
And hold lengthy conversations

Passersby see the beggar
See the Saint
They appear no different
To the worldly eye

How then can it be told
Your plans for your life
May be earned by your hard work
Or lovingly unfolded by
Angels of grace
Either way appears the same
Who then can see
The beggar or the Saint?

The beggars will admonish you
You must earn your living
Go forth, work hard
Succeed

The Saints have shown us the way
They have told us again and again
Seek not success in the world
It is not what you do
It all looks the same
It is who you are as you do it

There is a simple key
It's like opening a little cabinet door
You expect to find
A confined space inside
Yet somehow, as the door swings open
You are presented with
Grand vistas
As far as the eye can see
Whole worlds lay beyond
This door

In fact
Beyond the little door
Opened by this simple key
Lay all experience
All you see, hear, touch, smell, feel, think, and can perceive
A world encompassing
All your awareness
This simple key
Is the holy grail
It is the golden chalice
It is the treasure sought
By all worthy quests

The beggar's act of begging
Is the beggar's search
All souls pick up a begging bowl
And walk the beggar's road
So they may experience
The quest for themselves
It remains a paradox
That beggars are Saints in disguise
Who wear the disguise so well
They think and act and live
As beggars

Into the bowl appear
A shining key of gold
The act of begging
Had finally produced it
From where it comes
Remains a mystery
Not needing to be known

Awareness of the key
First dawns light
The beggar sees himself
The choosing of the key
Begins the path
Eyes begin to open
The turning of the key begins

To the Saint
Loving is simply breathing
The breath comes with ease
It is ordinary
It is no miracle

This breath
A natural though vital
Act of life
This key is pervasive
For the Saint
It is the stuff
Of life

Beggars and Saints
This mystery of our journey
The appearance of the key
Is no secret
Yet remains great mystery

If you see a beggar be kind
If you are a beggar be kinder still
If you find a Saint
Listen closely
And observe your beggar's cloth
Bleach white

Observe the mystery
How the kindness and caring
All men
Saints make!

Halls Of Grace

These most perfect moments
In the halls of grace
Sweep clean the debris
Of ill lived life

And glistening white marble
Glowing golden domes
Reverent devoted prayers
Are but the doorway

My entrance into grace
Has no beginning
For all that came before
Is now balanced in
This eternal moment

My passage through grace
Makes no sound
Yet in this quietest of moments
I hear life calling

Oh lover of life
Your love is this fabric
Of which I am made
A shining cloth clear and immutable

We have traveled far
Now rest easy
To live all your breaths
Within these halls of grace

Heavenly Sound

An angelic choir is coarse
And flutes are grating
When the sound of life itself
Returns unto itself

Butterfly Eden

As I turn and see Your eyes
I tumble into a loving
Where fragrant flowers bloom
And millions of butterflies
Cover me

Mecca Has No Place

Mecca is no place
Does the Maker of us all
Have a location?
And was the Lord born?

Oh temple of my soul
Oh house of many mansions
Ascend the spiral stair
Enter the upper rooms

Nor is Israel a nation
It is a state
Beyond ideals of the world
A chamber of the heart

Where did the prophets go
To collect the richness
Of their message?
To the streets of men?

What are the holy churches
And temples of the Lord?
Brick and stone, paint and wood?
Think again beloved!

The Holy One dwells within
Our beating heart
The Living Word has walls
Of flesh and blood

This clay pot
Holds the Living Water
A house here
In this world

Go where the prophets go
Climb the inner stair
The kingdom lies within
No building or location holds it

We make sacred a place
By our presence
Not the other way around

We give words meaning
Not the other way around
Holy we make a teaching
Sacred we make a book

Holy we are made by Living Love
Sacred are we in the heart
Of the Divine
We are living religion

The prophets and masters
Demonstrated this truth
Then told us so
Go within!

Loving is a simple key
Unlocks the tower door
The Maker of us all
Remains a mystery

Let go your study of the ways
Breathe in, breathe out
Sacrifice understanding
Go within

The loving between us
Contains the secret of the ages
Be willing to accept
The simplicity of that

It is clear to see
That ice is simply water
Be patient
As the ice melts

Amazing that clouds
Are water
Yet we know this
Be patient watching for rain

It is clear
That humans are divine
Be patient
As your ignorance melts

Amazing that our awareness
Is the Living Word
Awake beloved
Your awakening is the flood.

I Know You

You came to me
To sit before me
I opened to the mystery
Of One I have not known

As we faced one another,
Opened to each other,
And gazed into
Each other's eyes
Worlds began to open

In the unfolding moment
A chord filled the air
The sound of You
Your musical presence

A heady fragrance
Began to fill the air
So perfectly set
The heart of me
Vibrating in like kind
I knew You!

I gave You my words
Still, I tell You now
Inside my altar opened
Where creativity and love
Are birthed

And vistas of wonder
Began pouring from
These wells of plenty
Beauty filled my heart and
And began spilling from my lips

I entered Your eyes
As You flew in
The spirit of knowing
Flooded over me
I knew You!

Dear friend who I do not
Remember seeing before
Tell me how it is that
Your heart and mine
Our very being entwined
As the deepest of friends

As my words poured out
Tales of mystical love,
Spirit filled lives
And oceans of bliss-filled
Moments were exhaled
I knew You!

A companion to my heart
Fellow adventurer in this
Delightful creation
For a moment of endless duration
We merged

I admit I was swept away
And traveled to a life
Where we walked hand in hand
Best of friends, familiar lovers
I was at home in Your eyes
You let me in

Time flew during that round
Over much too fast
Yet somehow time stopped
And the loving went on
Forever

When at the end I held You
And then You held me
Our intimacy was simply
Freely given
And freely received

Only to find moments had passed
And the reality in this world
Was that I supposedly
Didn't know You
And we live wholly different lives

Yet in my heart of hearts
I am secure in my knowing
That the world of loving
We touched
Is as true and real
As this very breath

And the mystery of our moment
As well as its effect
Shall gently rest
Invisibly out of sight

Wild Dreams

I used to have a regular soul
Lived my tidy life
Crisp white sheets
Lovely dreams predictable

Sidewalks flat with measured cracks
Highway lines well centered
Parties with the in-crowd
Full of sparkling white smiles

Why now?
My dreams take a wild turn
Dump me from my bed
Sprawled upon the floor
I sleep with no rest

I dream of raging rivers
Ice floes creaking and groaning
Pile-ups high and bright
Train wheels clacking

Wake to find my bed sheets
Torn and messed
In the mirror
Some wild adventurer stares at me

Must be the winter broke
Spring thaw caught me
Tossed into the mud
Crazy eyed my pulse pounding

Those cookie cutter moments
The streets all look the same
I can't find my door
They all look the same

My key opens the lock
But the rooms are all strange
Whose home is this?
And who is that looking back at me?

I go out into the street
To walk with the strangers
Why not?
My dreams are no wilder than this

I leave what I have known
All I worked so hard for
My beautiful house
My well-groomed friends

Vodka martinis
Oh so shiny cars
I go to the street
To recover my simple self

Sometimes the crazy thing
The reckless thing
Is what sets us free

To follow the full moon
Across the sky
To grab the shooting star
To stay up all night with friends
Run naked on the beach
Kiss an unknown love

A little walk into the woods
Embrace the wild within
Wild dreams can bring
A brand new day

Thank You

Thank you
To all those who came before
To pave this way
Into
This wildly rushing stream
To walk upon the waters
With such elect

Thank you

Acknowledgements

I wish to acknowledge everyone who has been part of my life experience. My friends, family and acquaintances have all been a part of me getting to where I am, who I am today.

I acknowledge Nicol, my chief muse during the period when I wrote many of these poems.

I especially acknowledge those who have supported and stood by me, who are closest to me including my parents, Bud and Fleur; my sisters, Deedee and Hollis; Katherine and Danielle; and my beautiful kids, Kiara, David, Kumara, Dakota and Sophia. I acknowledge my teachers in Consciousness and Spirit, some of them being: Ellavivian, Robert, Ron and Mary, and Billy.

I offer the greatest and deepest of acknowledgment to my Spiritual Friend and Traveler who opened all the doors and showed me, in experience, the essence of loving, John Roger. I have deep gratitude for my brother in Spirit, John Morton, who has demonstrated to me the height of vulnerability, surrender and determination.

I acknowledge all the Travelers through the ages, all those who have shown the Way and all the mystical love poets who have not only inspired me but have given me *life*. I am grateful for my publisher and editor Tracee Sioux of Sioux Ink for taking me over this last hump.

ABOUT THE AUTHOR

Winston Hampton is an avid spiritual seeker, a poet and writer, energy worker and spiritual teacher. He began writing mystical love poetry at the age of 14. Win has spent a lifetime studying and practicing yoga, sacred sexuality, Noetic Aura Balancing, energy medicine, and Surat Sabd Yoga.

Win is well traveled, and holds a B.A., M.A. and M.S.S. He now makes his home in the Coloradoo Rocky Mountains. He has had many professions from couples counseling and parenting educator to furniture maker and custom homebuilder. He has spent much of his life married and has raised five children. Writing, researching, yoga, gardening and cooking are continuing passions, as well as spending time in nature.

www.ingramcontent.com/pod-product-compliance
Lightning Source LLC
LaVergne TN
LVHW051526070426
835507LV00023B/3337